PRAISE FOR *SELF-WEALTH*

"Heidi's approach is compelling and meaningful. Measuring 'wealth' can be very different than what you may think, and taking the time to read *Self-Wealth* will create a more accurate view."

—RHODA OLSEN, CEO, GREAT CLIPS

"Through the story of an extended family's journey, Helmeke explores issues of meaning, security, and purpose in life. *Self-Wealth* effectively serves to remind us of this timeless search in which we must all engage."

—AMY FLORIAN, AUTHOR, *NO LONGER AWKWARD: COMMUNICATING WITH CLIENTS THROUGH THE TOUGHEST TIMES OF LIFE* AND CEO OF CORGENIUS

"*Self-Wealth* is the ultimate guide to tending to your financial well-being. The benefit you will derive from reading this book is not simply borne of Helmeke's knowledge; it is also borne of her wisdom. *Self-Wealth* will tell you exactly what you need to do to get where you want to go."

—DON CONNELLY, SPEAKER, MOTIVATOR, EDUCATOR, MENTOR, AND CO-FOUNDER OF DON CONNELLY & ASSOCIATES

SELF-WEALTH

A simple, conscious path to a
comfortable financial future

HEIDI HELMEKE

ISBN 13: 978-1-63489-029-8
eISBN 13: 978-1-63489-030-4

Library of Congress Catalog Number: 2016931153
Printed in the United States of America
First Printing: 2016
20 19 18 17 16   5 4 3 2 1

Cover design by Andy Ross
Interior design by Ryan Scheife and set in the Whitman and Whitney typefaces
Author photo by Miroslavich Photography

Wise Ink Creative Publishing
Minneapolis, MN
www.wiseinkpub.com

To order, visit www.SeattleBookCompany.com or call (734)426-6248.
Wholesaler and reseller discounts available.

To my clients. It is a privilege to be part of your lives.

CONTENTS

FOREWORD

Happiness and Self-Wealth

I first met Heidi close to ten years ago and was impressed by her commitment to her clients and struck by her profound understanding of people. I especially appreciated the significance and importance she placed on her clients' feelings, experiences, and self-worth.

Heidi explained to me all of the specific things she did for client meetings. She was committed to not only their comfort but also their transformation. She wanted openness; she wanted her clients to feel confident and calm. She once shared she also wanted her clients to know that they were cared for and that they belonged.

All these years later, I was delighted to be asked to write this note but not at all surprised that Heidi wrote *Self-Wealth*. There are dozens and dozens of books published each year on personal finance, and this is a good thing. However, there is something unique and important about *Self-Wealth* and that difference is Heidi, and her unique and completely appropriate worldview. As Heidi shares in the pages ahead, her purpose, which is to enlighten and empower others, has made all the difference.

Everyone wants to be happier. Even happy people. Becoming, or learning how to become happier, is probably one of the reasons you bought this book. Perhaps you received it as a gift, in which case the motivation of whoever gave it to you was for you to be happier. *Self-Wealth* is as much a book about happiness as it is about your relationship with money and your personal finances, and this is why it's worthy of your attention. We all want to be happier, however it is our individual interpretation of happiness that differs. Everyone, it seems, equates being happy with having more money, as though happiness itself is for sale. This belief isn't completely untrue because money, in our modern industrialized society, is a tool, and it makes life a lot easier. There is no arguing the convenience of capital.

However, this credence isn't completely true either. We all know someone who has everything yet isn't happy. In contrast we also know someone, or perhaps many people, who have been incredibly unfortunate, yet somehow they are happy. Stress is the antithesis of happiness, and we are now, historically speaking, more stressed out than ever, even as our forbearers faced raging world wars, epidemics, civil unrest, and economic depressions.

In almost every measurable way, it can be argued that life has never been better for more people or wealth more possible than it is right now. We could even argue that our quality of life is getting better every day even though it doesn't always feel like it. When asked, the majority of working Americans reported feeling rushed, stressed, vulnerable and expressed concern for future generations. There are too few people who would tell you that life has never been better. Because of this, most people don't identify with being happy. Our lack of happiness is a national emergency and should be treated as such.

I believe many of us aren't happy because of personal debt and the stress that comes from carrying that obligation. We are the wealthiest society of unhappy people who have ever walked the earth. We live in big homes, and we own fleets of vehicles that we can't park in our garages because they're filled with extra stuff that has spilled out of our basements and spare rooms. Yet we don't seem concerned about this. Instead, we are concerned with what we *might* need or at least would *like to have* next. Heidi demonstrates that a key difference between happy and unhappy people is gratitude, and I applaud her for it. Her thesis is that true wealth comes from living a life of purpose and by doing work that matters and resonates within you in the service of others. Bravo!

Too many people believe that consumption will lead to their happiness, so they live beyond their means, believing that the happiness they buy will help ease the constraints created by living beyond their means. *Self-Wealth* argues that living gratefully and being more aware and thankful for our blessings will make us happier and is a wonderful step in the right direction. If you want to go inward, gain perspective, assert some control, plan a life of abundance, and live a purposeful life filled with meaning, then keep reading. And when you're done, pass it on.

—Dennis Moseley-Williams, speaker, founder of DMW Strategic Consulting, author of *Serious Shift: How Experience Delivery Can Save Your Practice*

INTRODUCTION

"There is no value in life except what you choose to place upon it and no happiness in any place except what you bring to it yourself."

—HENRY DAVID THOREAU

One of the most important questions we can ask ourselves is, "What do we want?" For each of us, that answer is different. We want healthy families. We want comfortable lifestyles. By far the most common response I get when asked this question is happiness. When I ask my clients to go a step further and to dig a little deeper—to define happiness—the conversation gets a bit more interesting. There's a shift in the atmosphere and often fidgeting in seats, and then I sense all sorts of emotions beneath an array of facial expressions—anxiety, fear, confusion. I often hear trepidation in their responses. Think about it: What does happiness mean for you?

The problem is that we have all received mixed messages about what we are *supposed* to want and what happiness is *supposed* to mean. So of course, many of us don't know where to start. Is happiness a prize we get after we've reached an important goal like a well-deserved job promotion or closing on our dream home? Is happiness a perpetual state of zen bestowed upon the spiritually centered? Or is it a changing phenomenon that morphs and shifts based on our ever-changing circumstances? Happiness dresses itself in different meanings, terms, and outcomes when we remove our basic needs from the equation. If we have the luxury of not needing to worry about clothing, food, and shelter, "happiness" can become a slippery concept often fueled by society's ideals and not our own. Ask yourself, "Am I happy enough?" and "Is there something that could make me happier?" and be prepared for an internal dialogue that might lead to answers that surprise you.

As a financial planner, I'm tasked with helping families achieve "happiness" through helping them plan for their future and acting as a guide as they pursue their dreams. If you're like any of the families with whom I meet, you've pondered this notion of the "American Dream." It's what our parents, grandparents, and great-grandparents all worked hard to attain, and it's what we're all still working hard to achieve today. But what is the American Dream, really? The more I've pondered this in my practice, the more I've come to see it as a rather elusive gauge of success and happiness. For centuries, the generations before us designed their versions of the American Dream. In 1931, James Truslow Adams defined the American Dream in his book *The Epic of America* as "a dream of a land in which life should be better and richer and fuller for everyone, with opportunity for each according to ability or achievement."

Through depressions, recessions, world wars, industrial revolutions, and civil rights movements, Adams's idea of "better and richer and fuller" has evolved. Today, we've inevitably and understandably entwined our happiness with financial success. When you factor how our culture depends on corporate benefits, government programs, and labor unions for its financial well-being, it's no wonder that the American Dream has become rooted in society's definition of success. We've become completely dependent on government programs and our employers for success, happiness, and ultimately, our fulfillment. According to the October 2013 Washington Gallup poll, "work is more often a source of frustration than one of fulfillment for nearly 90 percent of the world's workers." Our grandparents saved for a rainy day and designed their happiness around values and their dreams for future generations while many of us have skirted that responsibility and instead relied on corporations, the government, and unions to be our parachutes, dream makers, and life preservers. Even worse, in this process, many of us have lost sight of our purpose.

In the twenty-first century, we have more financial resources on which to live than previous generations, yet these resources have not encouraged us to save more. According to the US Census Bureau, the median annual household income in 1940, adjusted for inflation through 2012, was $22,434.61.

The actual average median annual household income in 2012 was $51,371. This was a time when wages were stagnant after the Great Recession. Middle-class families today literally have more than doubled their income from previous generations and thus have more disposable money to spend or save. However, the current savings rate in 2012 was only 4 percent. We're spending more, consuming more, and becoming less fulfilled even as our financial resources are increasing compared to previous generations. What I've come to understand as a financial planner is that true personal "financial success" means having savings. Also, I have not met a single person whose materials things (cars, homes, designer clothes, boats) have led to self-wealth. Material wealth is not enough for most people—to truly have fulfillment and happiness, we need to factor in work that brings us meaning, grow savings that can support us through the peaks and valleys of our lives, and establish a retirement plan that supports our long-term needs.

For more than twenty years, I have designed financial strategies for families building their life plans around the principles of self-wealth. In the process, I have seen firsthand the evolution of each generation's definition of success and happiness. My Depression-era clients, also known as The Silent Generation (born 1925–1945), have a healthy concern about running out of money and thus having to rely on someone else for their basic care and needs. They raised their Baby Boomer children (born 1946-1964) to have a healthy self-wealth by teaching with their prudent actions rather than words. However, those same Baby Boomers' children (now middle-aged adults) have different fears and different ideas about savings. They are less likely to expect a rainy day or have a plan for one, often living by the "life is short" philosophy and having a more carefree attitude about spending, which can be extremely detrimental. While I have seen The Silent Generation and Baby Boomers struggle with how to reconcile their savings-based fears with their adult children, I've come to the conclusion that the problem in bridging this gap has a lot to do with our cultural shifts.

I believe there's balance. The Silent Generation was on to something. We shouldn't let consumerism tell us what makes us happy, and we also shouldn't be oblivious to the worst-case scenario. Many of us are living the worst-case scenario right now: recovering from bankruptcy, foreclosed homes, a depletion of personal and financial resources, and unemployment pitfalls. But the other school of thought isn't all wrong either. We should enjoy our lives to the fullest and not *fear* the worst-case scenario per se. But what if we had a healthy combination of both ideals? What if we pursued our passions and designed our lives to have meaning—true significance seeped in the values we sincerely believe in—while also planning for a long-term and sustainable future?

In this book, you'll meet composites of real clients who have come face-to-face with these questions. You'll meet Kate Walters, a CFP® professional like me, who is counseling her Baby Boomer clients Clayton and Dorothy. You'll also meet their son Alex and his wife, Jess, as they begin meeting with Kate. Alex and Jess think they are doing everything right, but as the story evolves, Alex and Jess confront the illusions of their past ... and begin to embrace a new dream of happiness. By the end of this book, it's my hope that you'll have a renewed (and simpler) definition of financial freedom. I refer to true personal financial freedom as *self-wealth*—an empowering foundation, built around purposeful work, security, and hope, that can help you achieve the ultimate happiness.

PART ONE

Party Like It's 2004

JUNE 2004

"**M**om!" Brooke yells up the stairs. "Where are the granola bars?"

"They're in the pantry," I yell back, hairbrush in hand. "Did you have Dad sign the form for your summer trip?"

"Yes, he signed it before he left for work!"

It's another normal, crazy day in the Walters household—about seven and a half minutes behind schedule. I long for the days when having seven extra minutes wasn't an extravagant luxury. This morning is even crazier than normal because it's the last day of school, adding a whole different level of hyperactivity to already energetic children. Plus, it's now 7:36 a.m. and I have an 8:00 a.m. meeting scheduled at my financial planning office, before which I have to drop my two kids off at school.

I wrap up my routine, pull on my blazer, and go downstairs to corral the team—Brooke, who is eight, and Garrett, who is twelve—into our minivan. I enter the kitchen to find the typical commotion. Garrett is holding the granola bar above Brooke's eight-year-old head and looks down at her teasingly. "Hey, Garrett, give that back! Mom bought the granola bars for me!" Brooke says.

"If you don't figure it out peacefully, I'm getting the granola bar instead," I say.

"I was just kidding," Garrett says, handing it to Brooke. "I already had one."

"Did you let Ziggy out, Garrett?"

"Yeah, he did his business," Garrett says.

"Thanks, G," I say. We may be seven and a half minutes behind, but at least the kids are on top of things.

We pile into the minivan and begin the first part of the daily commute to their elementary school. As my mind wanders to work, the kids chatter away in the backseat. I feel lucky that they get along so well—most of the time. As I pull up in front of their school, I glance at the clock—7:47 a.m.

"Okay, have a great last day of school, guys! Love you!" I say as they unload their backpacks and lunches.

"Love you too, Mom!" they say, slamming the door shut. I watch them meet their friends in front of the school as I drive away.

As soon as I'm out of the school zone, my lead foot kicks in. It's 7:49 a.m. If I don't hit any stoplights, I can make it to work in six minutes, five minutes before my meeting starts. If I hit stoplights, I run the chance of bumping into my clients in the parking lot.

In my career as a Certified Financial Planner™ professional, most of my clients are Baby Boomers. I enjoy their attitudes toward saving and investing in the future; because the Boomers were raised by people who grew up during the Great Depression and World War II, they tend to have a saver's mentality and a strong work ethic that complements it. However, as of late, I've been getting referrals to work with the Boomers' children—*my* generation. In fact, my 8:00 a.m. meeting is with a couple named Alex and Jess Sutter, referred to me by Clayton and Dorothy Sutter, who are Alex's parents and my longtime clients.

I don't mind working with clients in my

generation, though I find it to be a bit more challenging. My generation certainly has more education than previous generations, but we also often have a strong "play" and "stuff" ethic versus purposeful work. A lot of our friends have an idealistic mentality about life; they tend to have specific, material checkpoints in mind that they use to indicate their success. This ideology tends to work against the benefits of their strong work ethic. Of course, Alex and Jess might be different.

I zip into the parking lot at 7:58 a.m., right next to a brand-new Hummer.

"Good morning, Kate!" says my administrative assistant, Leslie, when I walk inside. "Your clients are in the waiting area. I brought them coffee."

"Oh, thanks, Leslie. Last day of school ... thank goodness!"

After going briefly to my office and organizing my desk, I go to greet my new clients. The couple stands up, smiling.

"Hi, you must be Alex and Jess," I say, extending my hand.

"Hello," Jess says with a smile.

By the Rolex on Alex's wrist and the Louis Vuitton handbag draped over Jess's arm, it appears they are doing well financially. I guess Clayton and Dorothy were right about their success. I remember the Hummer parked in front of the building—it must belong to them.

I shake Alex's hand and then Jess's. "Nice to meet you both, and thanks so much for coming by today. Please, come on back to my office." I lead them inside, and we sit down; Alex takes the seat closest to my desk while Jess, giving another closed-mouth smile, sits down next to him.

"Alex, I've just loved working with your parents over the years—such wonderful people," I say.

"Yeah, they're pretty great," Alex says. "They're in Bermuda for the next couple of weeks. They invited us along, but we've got a Mediterranean cruise planned with our friends for April, so we decided not to go this time. I'm sure this meeting is just a formality; my folks trust you and wanted you to review our situation. But, you know, we're doing pretty well, and I believe I have everything in good order. I have a 401(k), and I'm putting money away."

"Well, that's good," I say. "Let's just talk a bit about what's been happening with your lives to start—"

"Well, my job's been going well," Alex almost cuts me off. "I just landed a new job as a regional sales manager for a local technology firm. It's a real step up. As I mentioned, my 401(k) is doing well. They match 4 percent and have stock options available as well. I'm making 20 percent more than I did at the last job, and I'm expecting a pretty decent bonus this year."

"Great to hear. Where was your previous job? How long were you there?"

"Before this, I worked for another technology firm for seven months—as a sales manager, not a regional sales manager. Before that, I worked in sales for two years at another firm, and before that, I worked another sales job at a different firm."

"Okay, so you've really moved up the ladder, you'd say?"

"I'd say so, yeah," says Alex. Jess looks at him and gives a hesitant smile.

"Your parents showed me pictures of their newest grandchild. Congratulations on your two kids! They're beautiful. I have two kids as well," I say.

"Yes, we had Colin last year. Haylee is four," says Jess. "They're such a joy, as you know."

Jess pulls out some pictures from her wallet to show me.

"Wow, such a beautiful family," I say, looking down at their four happy faces. "Where did you get these pictures done?"

"I found this great photographer recommended by one of the board members of Haylee's private school," Jess says. "She has done work for *Good Housekeeping* and has photographed lots of celebrities. We are so happy with her! We're actually scheduled to get our family portraits updated next week, since Colin is a year old now. We commissioned a portrait for above our fireplace. This photographer is so talented. I'll give you her name if you want."

I smile. "Thanks, they look lovely. What else has been happening these past few years?"

"Well, we bought a house last year that's big enough for us to grow into," says Alex, smiling.

"We have six bedrooms—a master for us, one for each of our kids, a guest room for when Alex's parents come to stay, a room we use for our treadmill and as an office for Alex, and in the last bedroom we're building a custom playroom for Haylee and Colin with a Winnie-the-Pooh theme. Otherwise, we've settled in beautifully. We have window treatments, furniture, paintings—everything has really come together," says Jess.

"I'd also like to get our garage floor painted before fall," says Alex.

"Wow, sounds like things are going marvelously for you guys. What do you do, Jess?"

"Since we had Haylee, Jess has been staying home," Alex answers. "With a one-year-old and a four-year-old, we decided one of us should be a stay-at-home parent."

"But I do volunteer work," Jess pipes in. "I'm the fundraising chair at Haylee's private school."

"Okay, that's good. Well, let's talk a little more

about your life plan. Alex, were you able to contribute to the 401(k) at your previous jobs, or is this a new perk with the job you've just acquired?"

Alex sits back in his chair and cocks his head. "Well, yes, I had a 401(k) previously, but I just took it out since it was only at about seven thousand with their profit sharing in the account. It didn't make sense to have an account sitting out there with such a low balance. And, you know, I'll be making a lot more money when I'm closer to retirement. Why not get the benefit of the lower tax-bracket now?"

Jess nods.

"Okay, has the money been spent yet?" I ask.

"Well, we used it as a down payment on Jess's new SUV. With the two kids now, we needed more space than our sedan offered," Alex says. "But Lexuses last forever; we'll get more than half of what it's worth new when we go to trade it in."

"Well . . . do you think we should still try to roll over the 401(k)? Can we still do that?" Jess asks me.

"Well, it looks like it's been more than sixty days since you've cashed it out and spent it on your new vehicle, correct? The IRS doesn't allow for a rollover back into a retirement investment after sixty days. Are there any other benefits to roll over from the other jobs you've held?" I ask.

"Yes, they all had 401(k)s," says Alex. "Of course, we ran into the same problems with the balances not being high enough to be worth keeping. I think the last move went to my Cadillac. Being in the corporate world, I need to be able to present a degree of success to my clients and higher-ups. Recently, I traded that in and got the Hummer. New job, new car."

"Do you know where the rest of the 401(k) money is, Alex? We may still be able to roll some of it over as she's suggesting," says Jess.

"Jess, we used the rest of my 401(k) last year for the down payment on our house," says Alex. He turns to me. "We wanted to have a solid home for the kids, and living in our old condo downtown was not a good fit. It didn't make sense to keep renting when we could be building equity." Alex continues looking right at me. Jess looks at him and then at me, her lips tight.

"Of course, having your own home is ideal for raising a family. My kids absolutely love to be able to play in our yard with the dog," I say.

"Oh, what kind of dog do you have? We're talking about getting a dog, right, Alex?"

"We have a yellow lab mix named Ziggy that we rescued," I reply.

"We love dogs. We're thinking of adopting a border collie named Duke at the local rescue where I work. I've had our kids come to the rescue to play with him, and he's wonderful," says Jess.

"Sounds like fun. Jess, did you work outside the home before you had children?"

"Well, Alex and I met in college, and at the time I was going into graphic design. I did that for a short time after we were married, but we knew we wanted to have kids right away. We also knew that eventually Alex would have a job like he has now where he would have to travel a lot, and it was going to be difficult for us to see each other with me working. So I quit right after I found out I was pregnant with Haylee, and I haven't worked since. Although, as I mentioned, I am the fundraising chair of the private preschool board, I volunteer for our local church, and, of course, there's my work at the rescue. All this volunteering is pretty time-consuming, so I've been thinking lately about quitting the dog rescue work after we adopt Duke."

"I see. Have you two thought much about plans for paying for Haylee and Colin's college?"

"Well, they will be going to college, and I would assume we would help pay for the education when the time comes," says Alex.

"Yes, I really don't want our kids to be burdened with student loans. They can be so debilitating for a young person. Our parents paid for our college, which is why we've been able to get as far as we did at a young age. I would like to do the same for Haylee and Colin," says Jess.

"Are you currently saving for this expense right now?" I ask.

"Well, we feel that if we take what we are currently paying out for private preschool, formula, a nanny, clothing, diapers, et cetera, we'll be able to redirect those funds to college when the time comes. I'll be making substantially more money at that time," says Alex. "Currently, my career path is set for senior vice president within five years. So we should be able to have plenty of extra money to fund college."

Jess looks like she's about to say something, but Alex pats her knee, and she closes her mouth.

"Did you have something to add, Jess?"

"Well…" She looks at Alex. "I have to admit that I am a little concerned that we don't have more of a plan to put money away now to help offset the huge cost we'll have when college rolls around. Haylee and Colin are three years apart, so they'll have at least one year when they're in school at the same time. And it's possible one or both of them might go on to grad school, and I want to be at least able to help them with living expenses while they're in grad school, even if we don't pay the tuition. I've heard about these 529 plans…"

"Yes, let's see if that might be an option for you. Can you tell me your current savings right now?"

"I put the maximum amount into my 401(k)

to get the 4 percent match," says Alex, "and I put six hundred dollars into our credit union savings account every month."

"Excellent! That's a wonderful start," I reply. "Can you tell me the current balance in savings?"

"Umm, I think we're only at about three hundred dollars right now," says Jess.

"What? Are you sure?" says Alex.

"Well, things come up that we need to take care of, and it needs to come out of savings," says Jess. "I had to transfer some of the money to cover the mortgage this month."

"Hmm . . . well, it looks like the six hundred per month isn't sticking," I say. "I work with lots of clients in your position, and you're not in a dire situation yet. But it's important that you make some changes now so that you're in a better position in the future. We need to work together to come up with a reasonable plan to put more money away and to cut back on some of the expenses you've accrued."

"Well, I try every month to build up the savings, but it seems like there's always something. We also just paid for the summer lawn maintenance, and we just had a custom swing set built in our backyard. Our neighborhood is big on curb appeal, and we take pride in our home," says Alex.

"I didn't want to put that on the credit card, you know?" says Jess with a nod.

Alex then turns to Jess and says, "You know, I don't think this is anything we need to be concerned about. Jess, the credit card will get paid off with my next bonus. I know you want to get our savings built up, and we can't do that without using the zero-percent credit card money."

"Can you tell me the current balance of your credit card?" I ask.

"We're at twenty-two thousand," says Jess.

"When did it get that high?" says Alex, a flash of concern on his face for the first time in our meeting.

"Well . . . each month we have Haylee's preschool tuition automatically put on there. Then your country club dues come out of there. . ."

"Well, I need the country club for my job. A lot of business gets done on the golf course," says Alex.

"And for the last six months or so, I've only been able to pay the minimum amount due," says Jess.

"If you don't mind my asking, what do you expect your next bonus to be, Alex?" I ask.

"It should be about twenty-five thousand in January."

"Okay . . . so it won't be a problem to pay off the credit card," says Jess. She's looking down at the purse in her lap.

"It's not a problem," says Alex, nodding. "The bonus will pay that off, and then I should be getting a raise at the end of the year. It's not going to be a problem."

"Is the twenty-five thousand bonus what you'll net after you pay taxes?" I ask.

Alex clears his throat. "No, but I had a smaller bonus last year and I was able to pay off the credit card. It will be close enough."

"Okay. I would recommend taking a closer look at your current expenses. After you've had a chance to do that, we should meet again to see how we could start funding some of your long-term goals for your life plan. Before you leave, we should put another meeting on the calendar."

Alex looks at his watch. "Actually, we'd better go ahead and run now."

"Are you sure?" I ask. "There're a couple more things I was hoping to touch on today."

"Yeah," Alex replies. "Sorry, we're going to be late for another engagement if we don't get a move on."

"Well, how does meeting in two months sound?"

"That sounds great," Jess says quickly.

"Okay, I'll give you a call later in the week to set it up," I say.

"Great. Thanks for your time today," Alex says as they stand up to leave.

DISCUSSION

Within the next two months, Alex and Jess will have more to review than just the expense sheet Kate asks them to put together. Alex and Jess have developed financial habits over a long period that are going to cost them. Of course, like most of us, Alex and Jess want to be successful and happy. But what exactly does happiness truly mean for them? Do they have self-wealth? And more, how do they achieve it beyond a surface level as circumstances and standards of happiness evolve?

At the beginning of the meeting, did you notice that when Kate asked Alex and Jess about their lives, Alex immediately talked about his career, salary, and impressive benefits package? As Kate followed his lead, we learned that Alex has moved from one position to the next in pursuit of pay raises and promotions. Alex never mentioned once what his actual job responsibilities were for his new position or what he enjoyed about his career. With Jess's hesitant smile after Kate mentions moving up the ladder, we see a glimpse of her insecurity with all Alex's job changes.

It's possible that Jess may not even realize her insecurity about this. Is the affluent lifestyle Alex is pursuing more attractive than the gnawing gut feeling she has about his career path and the strength of his financial, emotional, and professional security? Jess clearly has a desire to contribute to their family too and wants a purpose of her own, which might be why beautiful photographs, buying the new home, and having it decorated are important to her. She wants to *believe* they are doing well and are financially secure. However, we see that things are not what they appear, and although Jess wishes they were, she's probably aware that things need to change. When Jess responded to the credit card question with reluctance, we can see that there's possible fear about Alex's evident lack of concern about their finances. Yet Jess is looking for Kate to point Alex in the right direction so that she doesn't have to. Jess, like many of us when it comes to our finances, wants a magic answer that will provide security without forcing her to make any major life changes. Unfortunately, that's not possible. When it comes to achieving security, there is no magic bullet. It's simple: we need to spend less than what we make. One of the most common mistakes in this area is purchasing too much house.

We see this with Alex as he views the purchase of their dream home as validation of his success and likely his overall happiness. One might even say that he's overcompensating. What is Alex truly chasing in his pursuit of luxurious and expensive items? If we look at the housing crisis that started in the early 2000s, Alex's story is one of many. The outrageous increase of homebuyers with mortgages that exceeded their incomes became the norm. We know now that many of those buyers learned tragically life-altering lessons about their financial security and likely about their own self-wealth. It used to be that owning your own home was the ultimate symbol of independence and gratification, a sign of tremendous accomplishment, regardless of its size or features. Like you, I personally know several families who worked tooth and nail to pay all of their bills *and* to keep their home in times of financial crisis. One of our current dilemmas still, however, is this idea of the size of a home as a symbol of success—which, incidentally, is a relatively new concept.

When it comes to Alex's current job, I'm not sure he's sincerely confident in his ability to work through challenges he may encounter at work. In fact, it appears that once he's faced with a challenge, he moves on to a new position or company. Notice Alex's language. He often defaults to excuses and rationalizations for why he takes the road of least resistance. Does Alex have a sense of purpose? What is Alex afraid of? Like many of us, he might be afraid of failure or, even more, what he *perceives* as failure. On the surface he seems put together. Yet there still appears to be insecurity brewing beneath his outward confidence. What is at the core of that insecurity? For Alex, it might be that he cares more about what other people think about him than what would truly make him happy. He wants Kate to validate his decisions so that he doesn't have to face and ask himself tough questions—after all, as a professional, if she agrees with him, then he must be doing everything right.

What I find most troubling about Alex is the lack of passion in his work. He seems more concerned about the next raise, the next move up the corporate ladder—he seems more motivated by money than his purpose. I've found that everyone from plumbers to brain surgeons need to feel like their work is valuable to those they serve. My clients who are only motivated by money never have contentment in their jobs. It's hard to be happy with yourself based on your monetary value. I like what Eric Greitens says about this in his book *Resilience*:

We are meant to have worthy work to do. If we aren't allowed to struggle for something worthwhile, we'll never grow in resilience, and we'll never experience complete happiness.

Someone will always make more money than you. Bill Gates was named the richest man in the world in 2013; the last time he had held that title was in 2007. What happened between 2008 and 2012? He kept working because it wasn't that distinction that motivated him; it was his passion for what he does. Self-wealth requires purpose. Without it, we amass stuff instead of mementos and jobs instead of vocations.

I'm not surprised that Alex and Jess cashed out Alex's 401(k). This is common because most people have a hard time forecasting the long-term rewards of compounding interest. For many of us, it seems like it takes too long. Buying the new car now is preferred to having a small amount saved to go toward retirement.

> **Compound interest** is interest added to the principal of a deposit or loan so that the added interest also earns interest from then on. This addition of interest to the principal is called *compounding*.

At age twenty-six, Alex had two 401(k)s totaling $13,000 tax deferred (no taxes are due until the funds are withdrawn from the account). This would mean that all of the interest would get added back to the account every year until retirement at age sixty-five.

Value of Compounding Interest

13,000 (present value of 401(k))

6 percent interest (rate earned each year)

65 (age at retirement) – 26 (current age)

= 39 years until retirement

Value of $13,000 at retirement = $126,145.60

So the decision to cash out their 401(k)s and buy their Lexus SUV and Cadillac Escalade cost their retirement $126,145.60.

"Compound interest is the eighth wonder of the world. He who understands it, earns it ... he who doesn't ... pays it."

—ALBERT EINSTEIN

Having a car loan in the last decade has evolved from being the exception to becoming the rule. Just as compound interest can benefit in the long term if you are saving money, it will also work against you when you are borrowing money. Always remember that the institution that is giving the money for the purchase is in a for-profit business. Alex and Jess fell into the current norm with not just one but two car loans.

Look at the box below to see the numbers that support the actual cost of purchasing the two cars.

Interest cost on car loans

Original loan amount is $40,000 for each vehicle

Term (length of loan) is 5 years

Interest rate is 5 percent

Payment is $754.85/month

Over 5 years the total paid is $45,291.00

Interest cost = $5,291.00/vehicle

Amortization is the paying off of debt with a fixed repayment schedule in regular installments over a period of time. Consumers are most likely to encounter amortization with a mortgage or car loan.

If we look at the total cost to Alex and Jess's financial future of these two vehicles, we need to add the cost of the 401(k) withdrawals and the interest paid on the loans.

Total Cost of Vehicles

$126,145.60 (Lost retirement savings)

$10,582.00 (Loan interest paid)

$90,000 (List price of both vehicles)

= **$226,727.60 (Total paid for the two vehicles)**

Those are expensive vehicles. The bank interest alone increases the vehicles actual cost, negating the theory that using the bank's money is a smart personal financial decision. So what was Alex looking for with the types of vehicles they purchased? His comment about needing to look the part seems to align with a certain expectation about what he *thinks* he *should* drive—not what he can afford to drive. How much power should a piece of metal have? Does Alex believe that, because he is smart and has a great job, he can afford those expensive vehicles?

Once Alex's and Jess's car loans are finally paid off, their cars are likely going to be in need of repair or might not reflect their future needs at all. The big question: What would Alex think about himself if he were to downsize to having less expensive cars that were as durable, safe, and enjoyable for him to drive as his luxury vehicles?

One of Alex's reasons for taking the money out of the 401(k) was the theory that in retirement he and Jess will be in a higher tax bracket than today. Let's see if that theory can beat compounding interest.

Low Tax Rate Theory

Alex's Early Withdrawal from his 401(k)

Tax bracket now = 30 percent

Account value = $13,000

Withdraw $13,000

Cost in taxes = $3,900

Balance in retirement account = $0

High Tax Rate Theory

Alex's Normal Withdrawal from his 401(k) at Retirement

Tax bracket at retirement = 40 percent

Account value = $126,145.60.

Withdraw $13,000

Cost in taxes = $5,200

Balance in retirement account = $113,145.60

As you can see, Albert Einstein was correct in his theory regarding compounding interest. It had a much bigger impact on Alex and Jess's financial success than the potential $1,300 tax savings in the future.

The third issue, also common, is credit card debt. The assumption that everyone needs to establish credit has ballooned to becoming the new way of life. Unfortunately, people will only get behind in their finances unless they pay the bill off each month.

When there are two car loans that are $754.85/month plus a house payment and no savings, it is common to see people use credit cards for emergencies. This leads to not being able to pay those cards off or catch up because they are living above their income with no extra money each month.

Right now Jess and Alex are spending money they think they will have in the future. However, the interest accrued in the meantime by living this way will be why Alex's bonus will not be enough to pay off that credit card.

Credit card Interest

Balance on credit card = $22,000

15 percent interest charged monthly

Total interest paid for a year is $3,536.60

Education for their children, Haylee and Colin, is very important to Alex and Jess. Today, having a college education is viewed by an overwhelming majority as the requirement to getting a well-paying job. Similarly, previous generations viewed a high school diploma in this way. A majority of Depression-era children were lucky to finish sixth grade before joining the workforce to help their families make ends meet. The major difference now is that a high school diploma was funded with tax dollars and college is a private business. College tuition costs have increased faster than any other household expense in recent decades. As a comparison, the cost of medical care has increased over the last thirty years at 10.64 percent per year versus tuition at 22.19 percent (source: BLS, Consumer Price Index). Colleges are spending more to attract students, hiring more professors to reduce student-to-faculty ratios, and receiving less financial support from cash-strapped states.

Alex and Jess came from families where each parent's company provided for part of their retirement in the form of a pension. At the time Clayton and Dorothy were looking for jobs, more companies were also competing to hire employees. They started offering benefits including profit sharing, stock options, and employer stock purchase plans. Those benefits, paired with employer-sponsored retirement plans and Social Security, meant there was more disposable income and more money to help pay for their children's expenses, including college education. Alex and Jess do not have the same benefits and will need to depend mostly on their own funds for retirement. This will take money out of their day-to-day cash flow and restrict what they will be able to provide for their children. Currently, Alex and Jess need to make their finances the priority before they can focus on providing for their children's college tuition.

Another challenge is that Kate doesn't even have a chance to ask how much, if any, life insurance Alex and Jess have protecting their family. If you don't have enough life insurance, it's not possible to have the security necessary for self-wealth. In 2015, 37 percent of parents with children at home under the age of eighteen did not own any life insurance, either individually or via group coverage through their employer (source: Bankrate.com). There may be a number of reasons for this. There is still a notion that encourages us to "live today and not worry about tomorrow," which has resulted in the lack of focus on security for any emergency. This mentality has also contributed to the common problem of Americans being overwhelmed with so many financial obligations that there isn't enough money for life insurance. We should all be asking ourselves, "In the event of an emergency (death, layoff, etc.), do I have a plan in place to help my loved ones remain financially secure?"

PART TWO

What Matters

JULY 2009

"Garrett, I'll let you have the car tonight if you drop me at my book club and pick up Brooke from swimming," I say into the phone.

"Mom, Lindsey needs to get a a new phone at the mall, and I told her I would take her. It's the only time we can go this week, and if we drop you off, pick up Brooke, and bring her back home, we won't have any time."

"Garrett, it's not our family's responsibility to make sure your girlfriend has a ride to the mall. If you want the car, this is the deal."

There's a pause at the other end of the line.

"Fine," he says.

"I'll be home at a quarter after five, and we can leave at six," I say. "We can pick up Brooke and Lindsey on the way, and then you two can be off to the mall by seven. You'll have more than two hours; that should be enough time."

"Yeah."

We hang up. My teenager had certainly been acting like a "teenager" more often lately. He has been begging us for a car. Jeff and I told him that if he were going to have that freedom, he would have to save up enough to help buy a car himself and cover his own insurance.

I glance at my computer to review my calendar. Today, I'm making client calls all morning. My eyes fall on Clayton and Dorothy's entry. Clayton has been battling vascular dementia for the past two years, coupled with cancer this past year. I know that he is highly concerned about leaving Dorothy alone. I pick up the phone and dial.

"Hello?" a woman's voice answers.

"Hello, this is Kate Walters from Live & Thrive Financial Management. May I speak with Dorothy, please?"

"Oh, Kate, thank you so much for calling. This is Jess Sutter, Clayton and Dorothy's daughter-in-law. My husband is their son, Alex."

"Oh, of course. How are you?"

"Well . . . we've all been better. Clayton died last night, so I know Dorothy will want to meet with you, but she might need a few days before putting something on the calendar."

"Even though Clayton's death was expected, it's always shocking when they finally take their last breath," I respond. "I will always remember Clayton's infectious laugh."

"Yes, he was a wonderful grandfather for our kids," says Jess.

"You guys have enough on your plate right now. I will make sure those things that have time restrictions or deadlines happen on time. For the next few days, take care of each other and handle the decisions that are right in front of you. I'll call you next week when all the immediate tasks are over and you've had a minute to catch your breath."

"Thank you." Jess pauses for a moment. "Anyway, I'm sure Dorothy will be glad to hear from you next week."

Two months later, Dorothy is finally able to come to my office for her meeting, rescheduling twice before coming in. It didn't sound on the phone as though Dorothy thought Alex and Jess would be present, but as I peek out the window of my office, I see all three of them getting out of a dated SUV. It would seem that Alex and Jess decided to downsize.

Leslie shows them into my office. "It's good to see you all again," I say. I nod to Leslie to shut the door as she exits. "Please, have a seat."

Dorothy, looking sad and nostalgic, takes the seat closest to my desk. Alex takes the next closest chair, and Jess takes the chair by the door. I glance down at a recent picture on my desk of my family on a camping trip at the end of June. When I look back to the three people in front of me, I have to admit that they look miserable.

"Dorothy, before we even get started on business, this has to be one of the most difficult things you've ever been through. Would you like to tell me what you're experiencing now?"

"Thank you, dear," Dorothy says. "It has been sad and lonely these couple of months. My husband touched so many lives. Boy, he sure did know how to make life fun. He worked hard, and he didn't need anything to have a good time."

"I always enjoyed Clayton. Having known him for twenty years, I am so grateful that I shared in the celebration of his life. I loved his brother's eulogy—hearing the stories of mischief they would get into with the bike they shared. It brought to mind the stories my father always shared about his childhood. He certainly always found a way to make his own happiness and fun."

"He was a remarkable man," says Jess. She looks at Alex uncomfortably.

"We've been spending a lot of time at my folks' place since my father became sick," Alex says.

"Being around family can be so healing in these times," I say.

"Alex has been wonderful through all of this," says Dorothy.

"What a comfort that must give you," I say as I turn to Alex and Jess. "Would you like to tell me how it has been for your family?"

"Um, it's been a tough year for all of us, but you know, we're going to be okay," Alex says.

Jess bites her lip. I can tell she wants to say something, so I make sure to make eye contact with her. "Jess, what is it like for you with all of this?"

"Well," Jess begins with tears in her eyes, "we're actually not doing so great." She abruptly stops and says, "We're here for Dorothy. Not us." Dorothy speaks up at that point; gently patting Jess's lap, she says, "Go on, Jess. We have lots of time for this meeting."

Jess seems thankful for the encouragement. "Well okay. On top of dealing with Clayton's illness and death, Alex has been laid off since last August, so we've had some financial constraints."

"Oh wow, that had to be hard. I know a lot of people in the same boat. Alex, tell me what it's been like for you in the job market."

"It's been tough," Alex says, somewhat defensive. "Right now, I'm overqualified for the openings available. Instead of hiring managers, they're hiring consultants."

"You could try consulting, Alex," Dorothy says.

"Consulting isn't secure," Alex says, "I need an-other full-time job that I can depend on. Plus, I needed to be there for Dad this past year. He needed someone to take care of him, and I'm thankful for having had the time."

"I'm sure he took great comfort in you helping him," I say to Alex.

"I know I would not have survived this past year without Alex's help," says Dorothy. "I really didn't want to hire a stranger to help me. When it got bad, I couldn't lift Clayton, so transferring him would have been impossible. Not only am I so very grateful to have had Alex's help, but I also love seeing Jess and the kids more. It was a wonderful, happy distraction."

"I was struck by the changes in Dad from minute to minute," Alex adds. "I would get glimpses of him here or there. One day about two months before he died, he looked at me and said, 'I don't know you, but I love you.' It broke my heart and filled it at the same time. It feels so odd to not have him here."

"That's amazing that you were able to experience that with your dad. My own father died unexpectedly a few years back," I say. "I always felt like he was invincible. After he died, our whole family dynamic changed. What has it been like for you and the kids during all of this?"

"They have been okay," says Alex. "Being nine and six, they don't comprehend much, and I am not sure they'll even remember much about their grandpa when he wasn't sick. I had been honestly discussing death with them, as we knew that's how it would end, but we did think we'd have more time."

"I am sure your whole family is grateful for the care you gave your dad this past year," I say.

Alex nodded. "I'm glad I could be there. Losing my job was, in ways, a blessing in disguise. So, to answer your question, Kate, I'm still looking for work right now. It's getting frustrating, but I'm confident something will come through for me soon. I want to get a job where I feel like I'm contributing in a real way. I'm just not sure a consulting job will fill that void."

Jess is quiet, but I can tell she's frustrated.

"While caring for your father is very honorable, an income is still needed for the family. The reality is that it might be necessary to depend on yourself right now with a consulting business rather than depend on a corporate position—since relying on the next corporate promotion is what landed you here. There's a lot of instability out there, especially for older employees and employees over a certain salary bracket. We're in a big time of economic shift; the days of seemingly endless money are behind us. It's more important than ever to create a secure plan for your future," I tell them.

Jess bursts into tears.

"Oh boy," Dorothy says. "What's wrong, dear?"

Jess just shakes her head. Alex is looking at the floor, not meeting eyes.

"We haven't made a mortgage payment since September," Jess says.

"You haven't been paying anything at all?" I ask.

"What do you mean we haven't been paying the mortgage, Jess?" Alex says, suddenly enraged. "I thought we made all those cutbacks so we *could* pay the mortgage—the lawn, the golf club, the Lexus, the Hummer, the private school, we sold the piano . . . what about my severance? Your temp work? Haylee stopped taking dance classes for this. Jess, how could you not be using that money toward the mortgage?"

"It wasn't enough, Alex. We didn't cut back enough. The minimum credit-card payment alone was two thousand a month," Jess says. "So I had to make a choice—but when I would make a payment on the card, the interest the next month would basically negate it. And once we got behind on the mortgage, it was impossible to catch up."

Alex shakes his head in disgust. "Wow! Jess, how could you not tell me this?"

"I did tell you, Alex, but you kept saying we'd be fine and you'd find something soon!"

"Are we losing the house?" Alex says.

There's a long silence, and Jess finally nods.

"Based on what you've been saying," I say, "It seems we have a lot more on our plate than just the estate paperwork."

Jess continues to look at the ground and cry softly to herself. Dorothy looks beside herself.

"Why didn't you ask me for help?" Dorothy says.

"Mom . . . it shouldn't be your responsibility to

care for us," Alex says. "This is the time for us to be worrying about you."

"At this point, we need to develop a plan to rebuild," I say. "Losing your home is a difficult, emotional time, and I can't imagine going through this while grieving your father's death. That said, a change of philosophy and your commitment to a rebuilding plan will allow you to eventually be in a comfortable position again. But big changes have to start now."

After a small silence, Alex says, "We're here, aren't we? What do we do?"

"Well, since developing your financial plan is all about developing your *life* plan, shaping your financial choices and savings around your goals as well as your day-to-day happiness, let's just step back from all these problems for a minute and think about things a little differently. Alex, when you talk about caring for your father, you speak more passionately than I've ever heard you. What did you like about it?" I ask.

Alex shakes his head. "I don't know," he says.

"Come on, Alex," Jess says. "We have to figure this out. You know she's right—we need a new plan. She's helping us find one. Answer her question."

Alex is quiet for a moment. "After I lost my job, I would go and visit my dad. I was moping around feeling sorry for myself. Then I would look up and see my dad smiling. I asked him why he was smiling, and do you know what he said?"

"What?" I say.

"He found a word in his large-print word find. If he can find happiness and joy in that little accomplishment, I said to myself, why am I moping around the house letting my mom take care of everything? She was carting him to doctor appointments, making sure he got his exercise, as well as keeping up the house and meals. I couldn't believe how much of a jerk I was being. I decided right then that I would help out more with Dad. At first, Jess was bummed about pulling the kids out of the private school. However, she went right out and got a job at a temp agency."

"Jess, do you like your work?"

"Yes, I do, actually. At first it was to save up money for the kids' tuition and get the kids back into their school, but I have to admit that I missed working," says Jess. "And you know, I do see many successful people doing temp work who also own companies and are doing what they love—some who don't even have a college degree," says Jess.

"Well, the world seems to be changing in that regard," I say. "More and more people are going the entrepreneurial route in favor of the corporate career."

Alex looks to Jess and gives her a half smile.

"Well, there's a lot for us to talk about here, and we haven't even gotten into the purpose of our meeting today. Dorothy, since Alex is the trustee, we need his signature on most documents for the family trust. Since we did not know he was coming in today, we only have your paperwork for the retirement account rollover. We can get that all signed today. Alex, are you able to make another appointment to come back to sign your forms? And also for you and Jess to begin establishing a comprehensive life plan?"

"Absolutely, Jess and I will come back to do that."

"Wonderful. How does next Monday look for you both? Three o'clock?"

"We'll be here," says Jess.

"Is that all right with you, Mom?" Alex says.

"Oh that would be great," Dorothy says. "I am ready to go home. Speaking of home, I want you all to move in with me," Dorothy says. "I mean it. We have more than enough room, you can save money, and I can babysit while the two of you are figuring out work. Besides, it would be great to have a full house again."

Alex and Jess look at each other. "We'd love that, Dorothy," Jess says.

"Thank you, Mom," Alex says.

The following Monday, Alex and Jess return for their private meeting.

"Good to see you both again," I say. "Welcome back."

"Yes, thanks for finding the time to meet with us. Do you have the papers for me to sign?" Alex says.

"Here they are. Leslie marked every place that you need to sign. It is the same paperwork that we went through with your mom; it's just titled in the family trust. Jess, while he is signing, tell me more about what you and the kids have been up to."

"Well, I don't spend much time with the kids these days. Alex is at home now, and I am working close to fifty hours a week at the temp agency. It's been great; I'm feeling motivated. My last job was working as a graphic designer for an ad agency, but that was before Haylee was born. I forgot how much I loved to see how the business was growing and what it felt like when the clients were pleased with the work. I don't regret not working for their first years, but we just never adjusted our lifestyle to having only one salary. Had I kept working, we could have avoided the situation we're now in. Plus, I do miss graphic design."

"Well, that is what you got your degree in, correct?" I say. Jess nods.

"Have you ever thought about getting into freelance work?" I say. "Many companies are outsourcing their design needs nowadays rather than hiring designers on staff. I would imagine it's a great market for freelancers."

"Oh, in my dreams. We have to get Alex a job and move into Dorothy's home for the time being. After we can get a new place, I can maybe think about doing something like that."

"You're really good, though, Jess," Alex pipes in.

"Yes, but you need to find a good job again," Jess says.

Alex nods. "Yeah, I know. I need to find something."

"Have you thought more about what your goals are, Alex?" I ask.

"You know, as unhappy as losing my job and moving into my parents' house made me, I have to admit that for some reason there is a certain sense of peace in knowing that I don't have to go back. It feels like there's an opportunity here to do something that would make me happy. I haven't felt like that in years."

"Well, it's true, it is a good time for a fresh start," I tell him.

"When I was taking care of Dad and traveling to all of his appointments, I realized that I like caring for those who can't care for themselves . . . It seems odd, but I felt so good when I got just a half a smile or a pat on the hand. There are real people underneath these illnesses, and I loved being able to see that. It felt like a privilege—to see this real person underneath someone the rest of the world dismissed because of illness."

"But that won't pay for another house or rebuild our credit, Alex," Jess says.

"Well, I think now is the time to try it a different way," Alex says. "We already tried one way. It didn't work, and now we have to start over. We can stay with my mom as long as we need to; she loves having the kids around. I think it's actually a great time to see if the things that we love will bring us to the point of buying another house or rebuilding our credit. What if you start your freelance business on the side while you're doing temp work? You could build it up and start scaling back on temp work slowly when you're ready. And I can try to get a job in health care or human services somehow."

"Well, that all sounds ideal," says Jess, "but we need more money now, not a year from now. Can you even get a job caring for the elderly with your degree?"

"Well, no. I'd probably have to go back to school. I could go to night school and still be home during the day for the kids."

Jess looks uncomfortable. "You are talking crazy, Alex. Right, Kate? We need to get our finances in order before we can dream of anything. Things are different now. After seeing everything involved when your dad died, I am not comfortable with the protection we have for Haylee and Colin if something happens to one of us," Jess says.

I interrupt, "That certainly can be added to your life plan."

I'd been listening carefully as they both spoke. The Alex I was seeing in front of me was a completely different person than the Alex I had met five years earlier, even a few days earlier.

"Actually, I think you're both in a great position to do something new and fulfilling. What do you have to lose? You've already lost the 'stuff' in your life. You have a place to live currently that you don't have to pay for. You have a chance to start fresh in designing your life. You're being forced to rebuild—and you can design it however you want. How do you want it to look?"

"I don't know . . . we always talked about the fact that I would stay home and Alex would do corporate work for the great benefits. I thought that it was our best option. It's been hard enough trying to get used to temping. Then thinking about Alex going back to school . . . it just seems like a lot to take on," Jess says.

"Well, Jess, you probably are not going to find next year any better. And the year after that will probably be even tougher. And you love design, right?" I say.

"Yes," Jess says.

"The money will come if you diligently exercise what you're passionate about."

"I think you're right, Kate," says Alex. "I guess in all the years I've worked, I never connected it to the end product. It was always just a means to getting the next promotion. Jess, you are a great designer. Just try it. Like Kate says: What do we have to lose?"

Jess looks as though she might cry again. "Well, we have a lot to lose, actually. I don't want to blow the inheritance from your dad. I just feel like this past year has made us financially doomed. We did everything that seemed right. It was what everyone else was doing."

"A lot of people made the same mistakes this past decade, Jess," I say "But now you have an opportunity to rebuild by doing what you love. It's time to learn from your mistakes, learn to truly spend within your means and place your energy in work for the joy of it—not just to be slightly better than miserable."

Jess just looks at the floor. "We are so far behind on our retirement and college savings. I don't know how we're ever going to live the life we imagined," she says.

"Then it's time to reimagine," I tell her. "Let's take it one day at a time."

DISCUSSION

I t's been five years since Kate last visited with Alex and Jess, and at this point they are experiencing the life lessons and difficulties of their grandparents' generation. They are lucky to have a parent willing to take them in who is financially able to do so. In the first meeting, when Alex is defensive about finding work, he is struggling with his previous ideal of needing a job that he can depend on versus depending on himself.

Jess seems to realize that not paying attention doesn't mean problems go away. Her vision of reality has crumbled, and even at the end of the second meeting she is still fighting to keep the dream alive of Alex taking care of everything. Like many of us, Alex and Jess became consumed with their short-term future. It's easy, especially in this day and age where we're being marketed to constantly, to become consumed with short-term wants and neglect our long-term needs. In adopting a short-term outlook on life and hoping that the next promotion would pay for current overexpenditures, Alex and Jess made the fatal mistake of not having anything saved for an emergency. A short-term mindset doesn't plan for life's lows like the loss of a job, illness or an injury, or any unexpected catastrophe beyond our control. In 2008, the average household saved 0.2 percent of their income. Our society has gotten complacent about the need for savings, and it's not uncommon to hear sayings like "Life is short, have fun." To quote M.W. Anderson and T.D. Johanson's book *GIST: The Essence of Raising Life-Ready Kids*, "Fun is morally indifferent and spiritually detached." In other words, what Alex and Jess don't realize is that the "fun stuff" that they thought they needed actually caused them the most pain, especially because it wasn't coming from within.

Further, Alex is frustrated with not being able to find a job in one or two weeks. The 1990s and 2000s created a job market whereby an experienced and well-educated professional could land a new job quickly. The term "mass layoffs," which is defined as at least fifty employees being terminated, did not even exist until after 1996. The term is now commonplace, and in 2013 the Bureau of Labor Statistics reported 1,301 mass layoffs involving 127,821 workers. Alex and Jess are not alone in their disillusionment. After the Great Recession of 2008, unemployment rose to staggering numbers and left hundreds of thousands without a job, not to mention scores of corporations without the ability to hire more employees. It's no wonder that even today many are still struggling to make a new life, launch new careers, and start over. However, Alex and Jess have another obstacle in front of them: their lack of financial preparedness. Alex and Jess have no savings, considerable expenses, and no long-term assets that can be tapped.

Let's discuss the first area of savings. Americans saved 9.6 percent of after-tax personal income in the 1970s versus 4.0 percent in 2012. In the last couple of decades, a savings account has taken a backseat to credit cards, loans, and the premise of making more money through investing. These all provide us financial resources; however, with debt comes interest, and investing should only be used for long-term needs. A savings account provides security for immediate emergencies and for major purchases that are not affordable with monthly cash flow. Buying something on credit that you cannot afford causes stress. While there is a need for most of us to have a job and earn an income to afford a comfortable life, we've all become more consumed with spending our money on "stuff," which I define as inconsequential purchases we make that absorb more of our money than we realize without adding significant value or long-term happiness to our lives. It's up to us to decide what those purchases are. They're different for everybody, but think about how much could be added to your savings account annually if you skipped the coffee shop on your way to work, cancelled the gym membership you're no longer using in lieu of walking your dog, and ate your leftovers for lunch instead of ordering takeout. In Alex and Jess's case, this would have helped them enormously because they had nothing in savings.

Remember, in Part One, they put six hundred dollars a month in a savings account only to withdraw it by the end of every month for expenses they couldn't afford. Now when they need security the most, their shortsighted planning is backfiring.

Currently, Alex and Jess are forced to give up those items they could not afford. The kids' private school, the country club membership, and, the most devastating, their home. Not unlike others in this situation, they avoided dealing with the reality of a job not coming as soon as it had in the past to make all right with the world again. According to the Bureau of Labor Statistics's Current Population Survey, in 2014, it took on average four months to find a new job. From 1994 to 2008, over half of the workforce was able to find a new job within five weeks. In the past, Alex and Jess could have gotten by without a large savings account to hold them over through a short period of time with credit cards serving as a bridge. However, we've moved back to a more traditional average of needing at least four to six months' salary on reserve in a savings account. In Alex and Jess's case, their stuff can't even be sold to provide them with income.

Alex, however, seems to be facing other realities too. Before, he didn't care about what he was doing at work. His jobs simply paid for the stuff that was supposed to make him happy. What Alex was searching for cannot be found through the pursuit of money alone. There was no internal connection between Alex and his work; he was job-hopping without purpose. Our work, no matter what it is, should provide a sense of purpose. Daniel H. Pink states in his book *DRIVE*, "Purpose is what gets you out of bed in the morning and into work without groaning and grumbling—something that you just can't fake." We are validated as people when we work for something larger than ourselves. This work may not even involve getting paid. After a day of hard work, there is an internal sense of being part of the world that no one can take from us, and this is actually something humans need. Purposeful work is essential for an empowered lifestyle. As psychologist

Mihaly Csikszentmihalyi states in *DRIVE*, "Purpose provides activation energy for living." As our country has prospered, employees' compensation has increased; however, work engagement has decreased. Meanwhile, volunteering is on the rise. Ultimately, your salary isn't going to drive your happiness as much as having a connection to purpose.

Jess is learning this, too, in her own way. If you notice, Jess is concerned about the children's college. She's invested herself wholly in their future. However, what she's realizing is that her own long-term future is bleak, as they have spent their retirement savings over the years on items that gave them short-term gratification. There is not enough in their long-term retirement investments to provide any hope for the future, and that includes the kids' college as well as their retirement. Jess is demonstrating her fear of the future by constantly pressuring Alex to get a job that will pay a comparable salary as his previous positions so that she can have her dreams for the future back. It feels like the bottom has just dropped out from under her, and in reality, it has. She will face the hard truth that life is not about what she has and where her kids go to school. She is also getting a taste of purpose with her exposure to the work force again, and while there is hope around the corner, it's not going to be in the package that Alex and Jess expect.

There is an upside here, though: Jess is regaining not only the desire to make a career out of something she loves but the drive to do so. She has always been able to rely on Alex's income, and therefore has settled into the role of stay-at-home mom while neglecting her own passion. The idea of starting her own business is giving her confidence not only in herself as an artist, but in herself as a provider. She is taking the first few steps in contributing to their financial freedom.

PART THREE

The Future

2016

"Hey, Mom!" Brooke's cheery voice greets me like clockwork. It's Monday morning, and our weekly call is one of the highlights of my week, especially now that she and Garrett are both out of the house.

"Hi, honey! How are you?" I ask. Brooke is a junior in college and with finals around the corner; I know she's feeling the pressure.

"I'm okay. I pulled back on swimming this semester, so that lightened my load a ton."

"I know that was a tough decision, sweetheart. But I think you did the right thing," I reassure her.

"Yeah I think so. I'm glad the holidays are around the corner. I miss you and Dad, and I could use a break," she says.

"And you miss Garrett, too," I laugh, amused. "Don't forget him!"

"Okay fine ... and Garrett," she chuckles. "How'd that presentation go for him last week?" she asks. "He told me he was super nervous."

"Oh, it went just fine. He landed that huge retail client, and Garrett will be working with them directly on their next location."

"Awesome. Go Garrett!"

"You should tell *him* that," I chide gently. Brooke and Garrett finally outgrew fighting over granola bars and have actually become quite close. But with Brooke's preoccupation with college and Garrett's new job as a junior architect, I have to remind them not to let family take a backseat.

"Anyway, we'll be looking forward to seeing you and Garrett for the holidays. Your father has already started planning!"

"We're doing the meal run, right?" Brooke asks.

"Yep!" I answer. For the last four years, we've delivered home-cooked meals to elderly singles and families in need. It started one year when Garrett came home and asked if I'd make an extra dinner for Mr. Moore, our neighbor down the block. Garrett knew from mowing his lawn that his wife, Sue, had died five years before, and with failing health and no nearby relatives, he'd likely not have a special dinner for Thanksgiving.

"I can't wait to do the meal run. Who's helping this year?"

"I don't know. But I can't wait to see you so we can talk about it more," I say.

"Me too, Mom! Gotta run. Class starts in ten minutes. Love you! Have a great day at work, and I'll see you in a couple weeks," she says before hanging up.

As I grab my coffee and hurry out the door for my first meeting, I can't help my excitement. Alex and Jess are my first meeting of the day, and on the phone, they sounded thrilled to update me on all that's happened in their lives over the last few years.

We'd had a few tough conversations after Clayton passed away, specifically at our last meeting when we discussed how to invest their inheritance from Clayton's estate. With $35,000 from the family trust and $10,000 from Clayton's retirement account, we worked together to come up with the best strategy for investing it.

At the time, Alex had started a new job as a home health aide. A large difference from the jobs he'd had before. I was glad to hear that he enjoyed his new job—although it paid less—and that he was becoming passionate about helping others. He'd even bonded with a patient that reminded him of his father. I wonder how that's going for him. Jess was also starting a new career path and had reconnected with her love of graphic design. She was even talking about starting her own firm. I couldn't believe it. When I'd first met Jess, she was shy, reserved, and convinced that she should remain a stay-at-home mom.

Since the bank had officially taken over their home when I last saw them, Alex and Jess decided to shift the money that typically paid their utilities to go toward lowering their debt, which I thought was a great idea. In fact, we even looked at their expenses and determined that their largest interest charge was on three credit cards: 11 percent, 14 percent, and 24 percent. The combined balances were a total of $25,000. Based on their debt, I suggested we take a look at their savings.

I remember asking, "Do you have any money in a savings account right now?"

"No," Jess replied. "We haven't started putting money away yet. On top of everything, last month we needed to fix the brakes on Alex's car and had to use one of the credit cards..."

"I didn't want to ask my mom for help," Alex interrupted. "She's already given us so much with letting us live with her."

From that discussion, it was clear that Alex and Jess were still relying on their credit cards, especially for unexpected bills. I knew that trying to build a savings account would relieve them in the future of having to depend on credit cards as a quick fix.

"It would be great if we had more in savings," Jess had said. "But even without a mortgage to pay, we simply don't have much to put away right now."

"Well, based on balances and interest rates on your credit cards, you could save $325 in interest expenses per month if you paid them off," I'd suggested. Alex and Jess had both smiled hopefully.

When I brought up what to do with the inheritance money, it was clear that at first Alex thought it could be used in the short term, which was understandable.

He'd asked, "What if we use the money to get Jess's graphic design business up and running?" I knew based on what Jess had told me that she wanted more time under her belt, so I discouraged that strategy.

But Alex pushed back. "Well, Jess is good at it, and I know she'll be successful," he'd said.

I told him, "I don't doubt that Jess is gifted at graphic design. However, it takes time to become established in any business. Jess made a good point when she mentioned wanting to strengthen her skills and gain more experience.

"Remember, the first five years of running a business can be very lean as far as providing net income to a household," I'd reminded them.

I then asked Jess, "Jess, do you think you'll be more comfortable knowing your family's financial needs are being met *before* you take the leap to invest in your own business?"

Jess looked a little uncomfortable but replied, "I think so, Kate. Alex, I'd rather hold off on starting the business right away." Another blow to Alex's short-term outlook.

"Let's look at making your monthly bills manageable so you can start a savings account."

We determined that their current monthly bills were $2,750 and that they were bringing in $2,700 per month with nothing left over. After a long pause, Alex, clearly frustrated, asked, "So every month we're still spending more than we bring in?"

"Why don't you save yourselves the $325 in interest every month and pay off the credit cards with the trust money? Then the remaining $10,000 can be used to start a savings account for unexpected expenses rather than relying on credit cards. The money you'll save from paying off the cards—$275 per month—can be put into this savings account as well," I'd recommended. "Those additions could even go toward a down payment on your next home."

"Well, what about my dad's retirement money?" Alex asked. "Should we use that for any of those expenses you mentioned?"

I strongly recommended that they use any retirement money for their long-term future. But at the time I noted the confused expression on Alex's face. He clearly wasn't expecting that advice. He'd wondered why he'd need to start thinking about retirement, for example, when he didn't even have a home of his own anymore.

"Keep in mind," I reminded them, "that the average life expectancy is eighty-five years old. Most people want to retire well before then."

"Well, yes, of course," Alex said, still visibly perplexed.

"So," I explained, "if you retire at sixty-five, you'll still have twenty years of bills that you'll need to pay. For example, the cost of food alone will be huge. Let's say you and Jess eat three meals a day in your retired years. That means you'll eat 43,800 meals in that time. If you spent ten dollars per meal from age sixty-five and on, you'd need at least $438,000 for food alone."

"Well, how much would we need to save, then?" asked Alex.

"That depends on what else besides food you might need during retirement: a place to live, medical insurance, transportation," I explained. "Those are just the basics. Most people also want to be able to afford entertainment, gifts, and travel— just to name a few."

Jess asked, "But won't we have Social Security like our parents?"

"Yes; if all the requirements stay the same, you will be eligible to receive a benefit from Social Security. The amount, however, is not intended to fund all of your current living expenses," I explained further. "You will be responsible for whatever Social Security does not cover." Both Jess and Alex seemed to understand this, but they sat in silence.

Right at the end, Alex asked, "How much can this

amount help us in retirement?" But, before I had a chance to respond, he took a deep breath and said, "Kate, I have to be honest here. Looking at everything in front of us like this, it seems like there's no hope."

I nodded in understanding. "Alex, Jess, these funds are the start of your future. Compounding interest and your ability to add to the funds over time are in your favor. Trust me; there's hope. However, keep in mind that you'll both need to think big picture and longer term."

⬤ ⬤ ⬤ ⬤ ⬤

That was about six years ago. About a month ago, I got a call from Alex and Jess that they had great news. As I settle in to prepare for our meeting, I see Alex and Jess pull up in a mid-sized sedan. It looks to be a few years old.

When they come in, I recognize right away that they both look fantastic. Though it's been a few years, they both seem very healthy. Alex has a bit of gray in his hair and mustache, sure, but he's standing much taller than he was the last time we met, and

Jess's eyes no longer look sad. She's dressed in slacks and a bright yellow blouse. She has a glow.

We exchange heartfelt hugs right away.

"Kate, it's so good to see you," says Alex.

"You look great, Kate," says Jess.

"It's good to see both of you, too! I can't believe how time flies. You both look amazing," I say. As they settle in, I ask, "How did Dorothy enjoy her bus trip to Boston? I haven't talked to her since she's been back."

They both smile. "She had a terrific time. Of course, she's not as spry as she used to be," says Alex.

"Well, that's to be expected," I add.

"It was hard right after Dad died. But with every passing year, she gets better," says Alex.

"That's normal in the grieving process," I add. "It's a very individual journey."

"I think Colin and Haylee help a lot," adds Jess. "They spend time with her every week. Colin takes out the trash for her and keeps her yard neat. Haylee helps with household chores. That's been great because she enjoys their company and we have our hands full these days."

"Yes, Dorothy always mentions how wonderful it is to have them around," I say. "She's given me tidbits of what's been going on with you guys. I can't wait to hear more," I prompt.

"For starters," begins Alex, "I'm managing the home aid company I'd started working for when we last met. I really enjoyed the work, and I started making suggestions about how things could run more smoothly, and they went over well. I was asked to be senior director about three years ago."

"That's really wonderful! How was that transition for you?"

"Well, they paid for my schooling in the health care field, which helped me feel much more qualified for the position. And once I had that, my previous work experience and passion led the way to the director position. My new position pays more, though not as much as I made when I worked in Corporate America. But you know what, Kate?"

"What?" I ask.

"It's the best job I've ever had. I love it," Alex says gleefully. "I'm finally doing something that fulfills me.

Every day is different. I love our patients, and I'm able to be creative with how we improve the company."

"That's amazing, Alex!" I say, enjoying his enthusiasm.

"I'm so proud of Alex," Jess adds. "He's not as stressed as he used to be. And even though it's not a big corporation, we've been able to buy a home, put money toward our savings, *and* put a small amount toward retirement."

"Wow," I say, genuinely surprised. "I have to admit I was worried after our last meeting."

"We were, too," Alex chimes in. "We were scared that we wouldn't be able to truly put your advice into practice.

"Well?" I ask.

"We're still working toward our big picture. We get it now. Fifteen years ago, I had no idea what a big picture was. I lived for the now and only cared about being happy in the moment. After losing so much and Dad dying, I started asking myself tough questions. I wondered, 'Am I working to own stuff, or am I working for stuff to own me?'"

"There you have it," I say. I'm impressed with Alex and how far he's come. The contentment on his face is contagious. He looks more relaxed all around.

"Tell me about your home that Dorothy keeps raving about," I say.

"We bought a small, two-story house not far from Mom," Alex answers. "It has three bedrooms with a beautiful backyard and finished basement."

Jess adds, "I never thought I'd be able to be comfortable in a smaller house, but it forced us to get rid of stuff we didn't need and don't use. We put an office in the basement and have fun every year planting annuals in the backyard. I love it."

"I'm so happy you found the right house for your family," I say, observing a barely noticeable frown on Jess's face.

"It wasn't easy finding the right house," Jess shares. "And it certainly wasn't easy after we moved in and began rebuilding." Alex sighs and squeezes Jess's hand.

Jess continues, "We knew before we bought the house that things would change. We were prepared for the discipline of staying within our budget..."

"Thanks to you, Kate," Alex interrupts.

"With the budget set, money in savings, and a new start, we thought things would turn around right away," Jess continues. "We were so wrong."

"What happened?" I prod.

"The biggest surprise was losing several of our friends," Jess answers.

"Oh," I reply, not as surprised as I'm sure Jess and Alex thought I'd be.

Alex adds, "At first we'd see them at the kids' recitals or their sports practices, but as the kids got older, fewer and fewer of our 'friends' were truly there for us."

Jess says, "We decided early on that I wasn't going to spend money we didn't have on coffee dates and dinners at our old favorite restaurants. We couldn't afford it and decided it just wasn't worth it. And so after a while the invitations dried up, the calls stopped, and they rarely visited."

"That had to hurt," I say, knowing how hard that must have been for them. "I'm glad you stuck to your guns."

"We had to," replies Alex. "In the end, we became quite close to a family on our block, the Cutlers, who we get along with great. They have three children, and their boys, Matt and Joe, are buddies with Colin. Haylee babysits their youngest, Sarah, so it all worked out in the end."

"We do a lot of Saturday night potluck dinners with them at our house," adds Jess. "And when the kids were younger, we took trips to the park, which were a lot less expensive than what we used to do with our other friends."

"Oddly, I don't miss spending all that money at fancy restaurants," says Alex. "I do miss the old gang, though." He hangs his head for a moment, giving it more thought.

I decide to change the subject. "How do you feel about the plan we made for your inheritance?"

Alex replies, "We realized that you were right about not spending Dad's inheritance money with a short-term outlook. We followed your advice and took $25,000 of the trust money and paid off our credit cards to save that $325 a month in interest and the $10,000 to start a savings account."

"Right away that shaved $275 off what we were spending monthly," says Jess. "Our goal was to move out of Dorothy's house, buy a home without incurring a load of debt, and, as you suggested, Kate, grow our savings so we could start investing for retirement."

"And?" I ask.

"We were able to build our savings to afford a down payment and cover six months of our monthly bills. And, as you know, we haven't had to touch Clayton's retirement account."

Alex adds, "It was hard, but we started thinking about the future. And Kate, I'm so glad we did."

"I am, too. So Jess, what about you? What have you been up to?" I ask.

"I couldn't wait to tell you!" she answers happily. "I launched my own graphic design firm about three years ago, and after a few bumps in the road, we're doing great. I even have a full-time employee working for me."

"That's wonderful," I say. "So that must have been the big news Dorothy kept referring to in our meetings."

"My business is actually doing so well that this year we'll have more left over at the end of the year than we planned. I can't imagine what life would be like after the kids are gone if I hadn't started my business!" says Jess.

"Wow! That's amazing, Jess," I say, overwhelmed with joy for her.

"It's my passion, and it's helping our family in ways I couldn't have even imagined."

"Really?" I ask.

Jess adds, "I know we thought college was a long way down the road, and now I can't believe it's only a year away for Haylee. She's interested in engineering, which is amazing, and we're proud of her. However, we felt sad and embarrassed that we didn't have any funds set aside specifically for her education. But she's not going away for another year, so I think Haylee can work for me, which will give us some help and allow us to pay her out of the company's revenue."

"That sounds like a wonderful idea," I say.

"We are looking at all of her options for universities and private colleges. She has exceptional grades, so I think she'll qualify for grants and scholarships," Jess explains.

"But here's what's cool," Alex declares gleefully, almost rising from his seat in excitement. "Colin and Haylee don't *want* us to pay for everything!"

"I have no idea how they turned out so wonderfully," jokes Jess, playfully elbowing Alex.

"I think I know how," says Alex, smiling at Jess, clearly paying her a silent compliment.

Laughing, I ask, "Tell me more?"

"Well they know we have a small amount saved for their college expenses *and* that we also want to be financially secure when we retire so they don't have to take care of us once they have families of their own. They get it. Haylee decided on her own to open a savings account."

Jess proudly interrupts, "She's saved more than $7,500 in the last four years from babysitting for the Cutlers and for others in our neighborhood.

She started babysitting at twelve when we still lived with Dorothy. I think seeing us struggle after losing the house taught her about being smarter with her money. With the holidays around the corner, she'll be busy with kids on break, and then next summer she'll work as a camp counselor. She's so good about earning her own money. Her independence is a blessing in disguise."

"We couldn't be more proud of her," says Alex.

"We're lucky," sighs Jess.

"Wow!" I respond. "That is terrific."

"And Colin," adds Jess, "has been mowing lawns and raking leaves to add to his savings account, too. Haylee has definitely rubbed off on him."

"Do you think Haylee or Colin would consider going to community college first to get their general credits?" I ask. "Many of my clients aren't hip to this idea, but community college students reduce their overall college expenses by more than half compared to students attending four-year universities straight out of high school."

"We're absolutely open to it, and so is Haylee.

Colin hasn't started thinking seriously about college yet. But we're keeping our options open. With Haylee's exceptional grades, I think she'll have her pick of affordable choices."

"I like how that sounds," I say. "So it sounds like you both are doing wonderfully," I observe.

"We've never been happier," says Jess.

"I never knew I could have this peace of mind, Kate," adds Alex. "If you told me fifteen years ago that I'd have happiness like this, I don't think I'd have believed you."

"Well, you guys did the work. I'm so happy for you," I say.

"We're so fortunate," says Jess.

"It's almost like we feel this need to share—to give back," says Alex.

"I know!" shouts Jess. "After the Cutlers both got laid off, we chipped in to help them with groceries, carpooling, and of course Haylee babysat to lighten the load. That experience reinforced how lucky we are to have the quality of life that allowed us to help another family in need."

Alex adds, "That's what it's about for us. We want to be able to live well for our family's sake, but we also want to use our experiences—and our blessings—to empower others and help those who need a helping hand. Haylee and Colin are doing their part and finding their way in the world. We're thrilled for them, and we're excited for us, too."

"You both are onto something with helping others," I say excitedly. "Our family is stronger, happier, and more connected when we're giving back."

"We have so much more than savings and a good financial footing, Kate," explains Alex.

"It's true," Jess chimes in. "We've got this charge within us to do more."

"You guys, I'm speechless," I say. "And that rarely happens."

Alex and Jess both laugh. "Thank you, Kate. Stay tuned. The next time we come in, we'll have even more good news."

"Question for you two: What are you doing for the holidays?"

"Not sure yet," says Alex.

"I think I've got an idea."

"We're in, whatever it is," says Alex eagerly. Jess nods in agreement.

"Kate," Jess says.

"Yes?" I ask.

"Thank you."

DISCUSSION

Alex and Jess have done the hard work of achieving financial freedom. By working through the three principles of self-wealth—purpose, security, hope—they have emerged with the confidence to fully live their lives. They are no longer tied to an overwhelming mortgage payment, car payment, and country club membership, which ultimately led to stress.

We also saw that Alex found his passion and purpose in caring for others. He's excelled at his job without putting in eighty hours a week and has also realized that, although his work is satisfying, balancing work with his family and other interests is also important. Alex has discovered that his passion for his work and connection to his purpose complement the other areas of his life. A 2012 report from Deloitte indicated that only 11 percent of U.S. workers have a passion for their careers. In the same study, 79 percent of employees that demonstrated passion for their work also indicated that they were working at their dream company, even if they weren't necessarily in their dream role. Passion leads to more contentment at work, even if your specific role isn't your top choice. Alex discovered this when he started as an in-home health aide and eventually moved into the position that ultimately fit his skills and passion. He finally felt connected to a purpose larger than himself. And the same with Jess, who also has more confidence now. Her work is impacting people's lives, she provides value to her clients, and she's doing work that she loves. With her thriving business, she's created financial security for her family and feels purposeful, and this has provided her with hope, especially because she's able to assist Haylee through giving her a job. Jess's business is also providing an income that can help save for retirement.

It's also interesting to observe how Haylee and Colin responded in a time of financial crisis for their family. They obviously felt the shift along with their parents and were forced to adapt to their new circum-stances. They instinctively pitched in. Babysitting and lawn mowing served several purposes—they provided financial support, encouraged responsibility, and, most importantly, dignity and independence. With their job earnings going into a separate account for college, they also now have some ownership in their education. Another benefit of Haylee and Colin's jobs is the experience of an impartial person measuring their work performance; this is vital as the start of a long-lasting respect and purpose they'll feel throughout their lives. Thus, Haylee and Colin are learning self-wealth much the same way their grandparents did—through work and observing their parents' decisions and actions concerning finances.

A client of mine, George Millet (1951–2014), whom I truly respect, wrote specifically about working as a fourteen-year-old in 1965 in his autobiography, *Unexpected Left Turns*:

> *I probably got paid about a dollar an hour, which was pretty good for those days. I needed the money, so I just endured the smoke and the dew and the early hours and everything else for*

six weeks, and considered myself lucky. It was
hard work, yes, but I would recommend jobs like
this to any kid. It teaches you that life is hard
work, and jobs like this prepare you for it. I
believe that kids who don't work, don't have an
appreciation for life.

The ability to live within one's own means, which I define as spending less than what you earn, has proven to Jess that the sense of security comes not from Alex's job promotions, but from having a savings account to keep from worrying about unexpected crises. When Alex earned more, she didn't have to worry about unexpected crises. Now, Jess and Alex's savings account, paired with lower expenditures, has provided a sense of confidence to take risks in other areas of their lives. Jess's budding business, for example, is something that brings her tremendous joy and purpose; however, without her savings account providing security, following her dream would have been challenging. Jess is also in a good place because she's created a source of her own security through her business instead of relying completely on Alex. Alex is also on the path to longstanding security and happiness now that he's not chasing bonuses and jumping from one job to the next.

Even in 2014, many still faced the same struggle with long-term investing that Alex did after inheriting his dad's $10,000 retirement account. Thirty-eight million of the eighty-four million American households (45 percent) that were headed by working-age people (i.e., not retired) did not own any pretax retirement accounts such as a 401(k) or an IRA (source: National Institute on Retirement Security, BTN Research).

When Alex invested the $10,000 six years ago instead of receiving $7,000 minus taxes and penalties, it brought him to a current amount of $68,484 for retirement. With Alex and Jess rebuilding their financial condition, they were finally able to pay themselves first and make it a priority to add to their retirement funds. We now see that Jess's business is taking off. The extra income from her business will be balanced between hiring Haylee and establishing a company retirement plan. Alex and Jess not only have hope for their future but for Haylee and Colin's future too; they're both on their way to a life of empowered self-wealth.

The overwhelming happiness that Alex and Jess have in the end is what I call the Enlightenment Stage. In the Enlightenment Stage, you have a strong self-wealth, which takes care of your basic needs and therefore enables you to find ways to share your overflow with others. In Kate's case, it began with Mr. Moore and developed into a meal run her family participates in throughout the year. Alex and Jess have found through helping the Cutlers that helping others and giving back offers tremendous reward. In Alex and Jess's case, they weren't necessarily gifting monetarily to the Cutlers, but studies have shown that the amount of a gift does not determine the amount of happiness (*Happy Money*, Elizabeth Dunn and Michael Norton). In fact, where we often see the greatest impact is through small direct influences, such as preparing a meal for a neighbor in need, running an errand for someone who needs reprieve, or merely donating time to a worthy cause or organization.

Peter Thiel, cofounder of PayPal, established a record of relatively small but highly imaginative philanthropy (*Forbes*, 11/19/2013, Howard Husock). In 2010, the Thiel Foundation started offering to pay promising college students a $100,000 Thiel Fellowship to leave school to start for-profit or nonprofit organizations of their own. This initiative sparked widespread public reflection as to whether the cost of a college education is worth it. Colleges and universities find themselves under fire for their spiraling costs, and the norm of a college diploma as the prerequisite for employment is, as a result, changing.

As we see with Alex and Jess, education for Haylee and Colin will need to be thought through. They'll need to ask tough questions. For instance, what are they willing to sacrifice in exchange for a college degree that will likely come with student debt? Haylee and Colin at this point have adjusted their goals to match their financial situation. With the amount of savings Haylee has accumulated prior to going away to college and with being open to completing her general credits at community college, Haylee has created a life plan that should allow for a manageable debt after graduation. The verdict is still not in on whether Colin will pursue a traditional college degree, start his own business like his mom, or pursue one of various other options out there, such as joining the military or pursuing a trade. He has the desire and ambition and has witnessed up close from his parents the result of having a job that you love.

In the 2014 and 2015 school year, the average cost of one year's tuition ranged from $9,139 for an in-state public university to $31,231 for a four-year private university. Room and board averaged approximately an additional $10,000 on top of those numbers. The average amount of student loan debt that a 2015 college graduate held was a little over $35,000 according to a recent *Wall Street Journal* article by Jeffrey Sparshott. Whether college is important in reaching financial goals, determining our purposes, and inspiring hope is still up for debate. I think self-wealth supports pursuing a vocation in earnest if one truly has a passion for it and finds purpose in it.

It might prove challenging to fight the urge to spend, especially when we can justify the expense as something society says we *need*. However, our money (and, frankly, our time) is too often our tool to enjoy something in the moment when we know deep down it's not something we need. We witnessed Alex and Jess struggle with this at every turn. With the overwhelming pressure from media, TV, Internet ads, phone apps, and services like Groupon, there is always something being marketed to us to buy or experience. Yet when we have self-wealth, there's something larger and more meaningful at work that cannot be contented through toys, homes, and cars. When your life is driven by a harmonious vision that works not only for your own good but also for the good of others, there are unimaginable rewards. Self-wealth doesn't promise happiness through consuming and spending to become "privileged." Self-wealth, instead, promises happiness through being brave enough to do work that makes you outrageously excited to wake up each day so that you can save and invest for the future. The American Dream over the last decade has morphed into being based on a compiling of material objects and status symbols. Today, true gratification comes from knowing that your legacy reaches far beyond your office, home, and family. When you have purpose, security, and hope, you have the power to inspire generations, communities, and tomorrow's American Dream. Our grandparents and great-grandparents had the right idea. It's time to get back to the basics of purpose, security, and hope to reclaim our financial freedom.

PART FOUR

Building Your Self-Wealth

YOUR SELF-WEALTH

When I've asked many of my clients whether they have or are working toward financial freedom, many think about the amount of money in their bank account, while others develop a mental list of goals they need to achieve in order to secure long-term financial wealth. Neither perspective is wrong, yet this is only a small piece of the financial freedom puzzle. Financial freedom is most possible when you have what I call self-wealth, which is based on three fundamental principles: purpose, security, and hope. You might have plenty of money, which provides financial security, and yet not have a strong connection to your overall purpose. Or maybe you have a strong connection to your purpose, but haven't invested in long-term goals—saving for retirement or your children's college education— that would bolster your hope for the future twenty years from now. You need all three if you want to have peace of mind, live your dreams, and not be bound by financial limitations—the true definition of financial freedom.

Let's look at the journey of Gail, a mother of four in her early forties who had never worked outside the home nor had any education beyond high school. She was not only emotionally distraught after her marriage ended, but was also living with what I call a self-wealth void.

She needed help, so fortunately she met with a financial planner, and together they decided that her journey had to start with the basics. They worked closely on what to do with her settlement money and on creating a plan that she would need to activate once her alimony payments stopped. Without a purpose, it seemed impossible for Gail to even imagine a happy ending in the midst of her dire circumstances. However, she took the guidance of her financial planner and invested her settlement money toward her future retirement; this was especially important since she was entering the workforce later in life and would thus have fewer years to build a company retirement account or have access to a pension. They then started to develop a savings for emergency funds. Every step they made together brought her more peace and understanding. Over the next few years, her confidence grew and she enrolled in a technical college. Though it wasn't easy being one of the oldest students in her classes, Gail graduated with honors as a dental assistant. Her life changed even more after being able to provide her own financial security. Gail found purpose both in school and now in her new career, which she loved.

She could easily have spent her divorce settlement on a new home, but doing that would have left her broke in five years. Instead, with some guidance, she chose the path that would sustain a future that provided far more hope than any emotional decision she could have made following her divorce. Her goal is now to retire debt-free at sixty-five; the long-term investments that she made will provide income to sustain her lifestyle for the next thirty years. Even more, she has also been empowered to help her aging mother who has Alzheimer's and her brother who has serious health issues. Gail went from being dependent on her husband to being able to provide for herself and others. Her life represents the balance needed to have true self-wealth. She has purpose through an enjoyable career that provides financial and emotional well-being. She has security from the savings plan that will provide a safety net in case of an emergency. And she has hope for the future from the balance in her long-term investment account that will allow for a comfortable lifestyle during retirement. With her strong self-wealth, she's empowered to continue her journey of giving back.

Before you measure your self-wealth, review the definitions below. The key is to think about where you are not based on your wants, which is where most of our inclinations lead us, but on your needs. What do you *need* in order to live a purposeful life that fuels security so that you have hope for the future regardless of life's twists and turns?

PURPOSE

I have worked with many clients who've lost their purpose. For example, I worked with a construction worker who, until being laid off during the housing crisis, was bound to his profession solely because of the money that it provided for his family. After external factors forced him to look for another job, he realized he'd always wanted to be a teacher. However, it required that he go back to school. In the end, he and his family were happier than ever before.

Sometimes people's career paths take them away from the reason they started working in that profession in the first place. A motivated female client of mine in the medical industry found herself at a large corporation spending more time communicating with and processing reports for the company's upper management than meeting with her clients. Realizing how far her job had taken her away from her purpose, she started looking for another place to work. Her purpose was so important to her overall self-wealth that she left $400,000 in long-term stock options behind.

I'm always excited by the large number of my clients who have found their purpose in their careers. However, once some reach retirement, it becomes a struggle for them to maintain their sense of purpose. For the record, "work" doesn't have to be a traditional job that pays with dollars and cents. The work of stay-at-home parents, homemakers, and volunteers is as important and meaningful as work that pays a salary. I have retired clients who are driving seniors to their doctor's appointments, volunteering at shelters, and dedicating time to rehabilitation centers. There are others who take what was once a hobby, like photography, and give it the nurturing it needs to evolve into a business. Of course, others spend their days providing assistance to family members, whether it's to their parents who may have failing health or to their children who need assistance transporting grandchildren.

You know that you're connected to a purpose when your "work" doesn't feel like work, or if your everyday tasks and responsibilities are joyful, challenge your sensibilities, and complement your strengths. Are you living a life that spiritually, emotionally, and financially aligns with your gifts? Are you happy with the work you're doing on a deeper level that has less to do with salary and more to do with fulfillment? Purpose is the foundational principle of financial freedom. Without knowing your purpose, the wealth you accumulate is likely to feel insubstantial, or worse, burdensome.

SECURITY

If you have a strong sense of security, you have the resources to rebound, pivot, or regroup at any stage in your life. We often think about security as having money saved for unexpected crises—an illness, injury, job loss, accident, or divorce. But having self-wealth also means having savings and resources for positive life transitions, both planned and unforeseen—getting married, starting a family, a career change, and buying a home. After your immediate needs are met (food, shelter, and clothing), what are you doing to secure your lifestyle? Your well-being is only as strong as your ability to adapt when changes and transitions occur. You should be able to change your circumstances, if necessary, without worrying about your immediate needs being compromised. Once you're living at a high measure of security, you have limitless flexibility and independence.

A stable savings account allows many of my clients the freedom to make choices that reflect their goals in life. For example, a medical device salesman has always had a keen eye on his savings account, which helps him advance in his career, which is commission-based. In fact, if he had not had a sizable savings account when he was recently challenged to move to another company, it would have been a much riskier move because he had to start a new client base. Instead, his savings provided opportunities that he might have turned down otherwise. Financial burdens and the stress of daily bills are not holding him back.

Think of building security as also building a doorway to opportunities for yourself. For instance, a client of mine was recently recruited by a firm across the country for an exciting new career opportunity. However, it was not a good time to sell her home because it was a buyer's market. Coincidentally, it was a great time to buy a new home in her new city. My client and her husband, fortunately, had enough funds in their savings account to afford to own two homes at once until the market improved enough to sell their previous home. A healthy savings account in this instance dissolved what could have been a barrier to a tremendous opportunity for my client and her family.

Most people realize that, once they retire, they won't have a check coming their way every two weeks. But many of them don't understand the true impact this has on their lives. They hold on to the idea that, if they need money, they'll be able to get it—but this isn't always the case. What happens in the case of emergency situations or unexpected setbacks when you need to write a check *right now*? This is why having a sufficient amount of liquid funds available—namely, in a savings account—is so important. It's impossible to predict for every future situation; the best way to prepare is to plan for the unexpected. This is the only way to give yourself and your family stability, therefore providing security.

HOPE

When you look at the current track you're on professionally, financially, and emotionally, are you optimistic about where life is leading you? Do you have confidence that your future will be as good as or better than where you are today? I believe your level of hope is inextricably tied to your long-term vision. Can you support your vision with long-term investments? For many of my clients, having hope can be as simple as knowing they'll be able to cover unexpected health issues, have the ability to retire, or have the means to help their children with their education.

Imagine a father of four who becomes a widower unexpectedly; his life plans are now drastically changed. He fears for not only his future but also for his children's. However, if he takes the proper steps in figuring out college funding, with a combination of avenues including long-term investing, he can eventually find renewed hope for his family's future despite his tremendous loss. Over time, his plan can evolve and shift focus to his retirement investments, which again can provide him more hope.

Now imagine a couple working toward a goal—let's say they want to own a cabin sometime in the future. They know they can't afford one now because they're expanding their family, so they work with a financial advisor to open an investment account specifically to make their dream attainable someday. Ten years later, they receive a timely phone call from a cousin regarding a family cabin that is for sale. Even though they now have four children, they not only have the money for a nice down payment, but they are able to purchase the cabin at a reasonable price with a loan payment easily within their monthly budget—all because of their investment account. These are examples of folks who understand their vision and positioned themselves to achieve it over time.

THE SELF-WEALTH
READER'S GUIDE

O nce you've outlined your needs with purpose, security, and hope, I suggest using the
Self-Wealth Score Sheet as a measure for how well
you're doing with your personal self-wealth. Keep
in mind that self-wealth evolves as your life evolves.
What gives you purpose now will not necessarily
give you purpose in ten years. The same rule applies
for security and hope.

THE SELF-WEALTH SCORE SHEET

Rate your level of confidence in each Self-Wealth statement on a scale of 1-5.

① ② ③ ④ ⑤

Low   High

1. I am investing either monthly or yearly toward at least one long-term goal I intend to reach ten or more years from now.

    ① ② ③ ④ ⑤

2. I usually pay off my credit cards each month.

    ① ② ③ ④ ⑤

3. If I lost my source of income today, I would be able to maintain my current lifestyle for at least six months without interruption.

    ① ② ③ ④ ⑤

4. I am investing the maximum amount I am allowed for retirement.

① ② ③ ④ ⑤

5. I do not have to eliminate any of my basic needs to fund a cause that I care about.

① ② ③ ④ ⑤

6. I enjoy the work I do most days.

① ② ③ ④ ⑤

7. If I wanted to change the course of my career, for example, by going back to school or starting my own business, I would not have to take out a loan to fund the entire endeavor.

① ② ③ ④ ⑤

8. My life nurtures my personal goals in a way that feels natural and inspires others.

① ② ③ ④ ⑤

9. I'm excited about where my choices and decisions are leading me, and I expect that in five to ten years I'll be exactly where I want to be or better.

   ① ② ③ ④ ⑤

10. When I am doing volunteer projects, I do not feel that it takes away from my own goals or tasks.

    ① ② ③ ④ ⑤

11. I have life insurance to pay off all my current loans and to help take care of my dependents/ family when I die.

    ① ② ③ ④ ⑤

12. The things I love most about my job have little to do with my salary.

    ① ② ③ ④ ⑤

Your Self-Wealth Results

29 and Under

It's time to consider a personal financial change. While it'll take hard work, dedication, and perseverance to turn things around, you can start with a simple adjustment today to bring about the results you're seeking. For example, do you need to create a budget and stick to it? Can you update your resume to secure a job in alignment with your purpose? Have you considered habits, purchases, and mindsets that are holding you back financially?

Between 30 and 45

You're on the right track. While you need to make adjustments, you've done a good job working steadily toward the outcome you desire. Be careful of becoming stagnant in any of the areas of self-wealth—purpose, security, and hope. Hold yourself accountable to the vision you've established for your life, and push yourself when possible. Now is the time to be intentional and strategic, to avoid the risk of becoming vulnerable to financial pitfalls. Focus on the areas where your self-wealth is lacking and where you are the most limited.

45 AND OVER

You've done a wonderful job balancing your purpose, security, and hope. You are also feeling some empowerment to give to others. Consider if there are areas that can be strengthened. To maintain this level of self-wealth, know that as your life evolves, so does your self-wealth. When in doubt, refer back to the Self-Wealth Assessment. As you've reached an admirable position in your life, now is the time to keep going, giving, and growing!

> When making any major financial, professional, and emotional decisions, refer back to the score sheet to measure how it aligns with maintaining or increasing your self-wealth.

It's Simple

Anytime you are faced with a financial decision, ask yourself the three questions below.

1. **Will this give me purpose?**

2. **Will this provide security?**

3. **Will this provide hope for my future?**

If you can't answer yes to any of these questions, it might not be the right financial decision for you.

SELF-WEALTH BIBLIOGRAPHY

Adams, Susan. 2013. "Unhappy Employees Outnumber Happy Ones
By Two To One Worldwide." *Forbes*, October 10. http://www
.forbes.com/sites/susanadams/2013/10/10/unhappy-employees-
outnumber-happy-ones-by-two-to-one-worldwide/.

Adams, James T. 1931. *The Epic of America*. Boston: Little, Brown, and
Co.

Anderson, Michael W., and Timothy D. Johanson. 2013. *GIST: The
Essence of Raising Life-Ready Kids*. Minneapolis: GISTWorks, LLC.

Barrow, Becky. 2012. "Workers In The 1950s Worked Longer Hours In
Tougher Conditions And With Less Holiday - So Why Were They
Happier Than We Are Now?" *This is Money*. February 1. http://
www.thisismoney.co.uk/money/news/article-2094769/Workers
-1950s-worked-longer-hours-tougher-conditions-holiday--happier
-now.html#ixzz3x9QEVlGL.

Bureau of Labor Statistics. 2013. "Mass Layoff Summary." *Bureau of
Labor Statistics*, June 21. http://www.bls.gov/news.release/mmls
.nr0.htm.

Bramswell, Jason. 2013. "Deloitte Study: US Workers Lack Passion."
AccountingWeb. September 24. http://www.accountingweb.com/
practice/growth/deloitte-study-us-workers-lack-passion.

Bromstein, Elizabeth. 2014. "It Takes 16 Weeks to Get a New Job."
Workopolis. April 21. http://careers.workopolis.com/advice/it
-takes-16-weeks-to-get-a-new-job/.

Choi, Janet. 2013. "The Motivation Trifecta: Autonomy, Mastery, and
Purpose." *Delivering Happiness*. July 10. http://deliveringhappiness
.com/the-motivation-trifecta-autonomy-mastery-and-purpose/#
sthash.L4docMk1.dpuf.

CollegeBoard. 2015. "Trends in College Pricing 2015: Average
    Published Undergraduate Charges by Sector, 2015-2016."
    CollegeBoard. 2015 http://trends.collegeboard.org/sites/default/
    files/trends-college-pricing-web-final-508-2.pdf.

Dunn, Elizabeth, and Michael Norton. 2013. *Happy Money: The
    Science of Happier Spending*. London: Oneworld Publications.

Hamilton Project, The. 2013. "U.S. Personal Saving Rate, 1970-2012."
    The Hamilton Project, March 14. http://www.hamiltonproject.org/
    charts/u.s._personal_saving_rate_1970-2012.

Husock, Howard. 2013. "60 Minutes And The Gates-Buffett 'Giving
    Pledge': What They Got Right–and Wrong," *Forbes*, November 19.
    http://www.forbes.com/sites/howardhusock/2013/11/19/700/.

Jacobs, Bert. 2013. "Do What You Like, Like What You Do." TEDx
    Talk video, December 19. https://www.youtube.com/watch?v=fZ
    B2vVHmiug.

Kamanetz, Anya. 2015. "Live to Make Money, Or Make Money to
    Live." *Chicago Tribune*, July 7. http://www.chicagotribune.com/
    business/sns-201507072030--tms--savingsgctnzy-a20150707
    -20150707-story.html.

"Live an Authentic Life: 10 Factors You Should Stop Caring About
    Today to be True to Yourself," Positive Provocations (blog),
    August 23, 2013, http://positiveprovocations.com/2013/08/23/
    live-an-authentic-life-10-factors-you-should-stop-caring-about
    -today-to-be-true-to-yourself/.

MacDonald, Jay. 2015. "Survey: How many of us have life insurance?
    And how many have enough of it?" Bankrate, July 8. http://www
    .bankrate.com/finance/insurance/money-pulse-0715.aspx#ixzz3x
    9BNdu6R.

Pink, Daniel H. 2011. *Drive: The Surprising Truth About What Motivates
    Us*. New York City: Penguin Group (USA) Inc.

Rhee, Nari. 2013. "The Retirement Savings Crisis: Is It Worse Than
    We Think?" *National Institute on Retirement Security*, June. http://
    www.nirsonline.org/storage/nirs/documents/Retirement%20
    Savings%20Crisis/retirementsavingscrisis_final.pdf.

Samuelson, Robert J. 2014. "Myth-making about economic inequality." *Washington Post*. February 1. https://www.washingtonpost.com/ opinions/robert-samuelson-myth-making-about-economic-in equality/2014/02/02/4cda72ac-8a9a-11e3-a5bd-844629433ba3_ story.html.

Schultz, Howard. 2012. "We All Want the Same Things." TheLeapTV video, January 30. https://www.youtube.com/watch?v=FT6EnlA o9fY&list=PL78CFB2E28A18CB96&index=6&noredirect=1

Sparshott, Jeffrey. 2015. "Congratulations, Class of 2015. You're the Most Indebted Ever (For Now)." *Wall Street Journal*. May 8. http://blogs.wsj.com/economics/2015/05/08/congratulations -class-of-2015-youre-the-most-indebted-ever-for-now/.

ACKNOWLEDGMENTS

I could not have written this book without the many people in my life who guided and shaped my own self-wealth. I would specifically like to thank my fathers: one who showed me every day that work should be enjoyed no matter how hard (and possibly *because* it is hard); the other who showed me that the world had more possibilities for me than I had ever imagined.

Thank you to my husband, Rob, and to my children for supporting me during the process of getting my ideas onto the page. Thank you especially for dealing with the constant stacks of papers and books on our dining room table and for tolerating the kitchen counter as my workspace.

Thank you to the numerous colleagues and friends who have helped with this book in some form. Thanks to Charles Blossom who provided tremendous support and encouragement with writing this book. Thanks to Dennis Moseley-Williams who has been the force that continually coaches me to avoid my fear (which he calls "The Lizard") and helped me fulfill my purpose in writing. Thanks to Katherine Roy for her time and also the research she generously shared. Thanks to Margaret Smith, founder of UXL, for continually helping me see the big picture and not letting the day-to-day interrupt the progress of getting this book to the finish line.

Many thanks to Wise Ink Creative Publishing and to Dara Beevas for helping organize my thoughts, ideas, and ramblings. A special thank you to my cover designer, Andy Ross.

HEIDI'S STORY

Heidi Helmeke began her path in the financial arena at the age of sixteen when she was hired as a bank teller. Her work experience continued while she was enrolled in the Pre-dental Scholars Program at Marquette University. After two and a half years, she realized her financial burden for college and then dental school would leave her with a tremendous amount of debt that, even with a dentist's income, she wouldn't be able to pay off until the age of forty. She swiftly changed her degree to psychology. After taking another banking position following college, Heidi worked her way to vice president and was asked to create an investment department. She immediately found her new calling. Her work experience with clients helped Heidi realize she wanted to assist them on a deeper level with their financial decisions and went on to earn her Certified Financial Planner™ certification.

Since 1990, Heidi has dedicated her career to designing personalized financial strategies for individuals looking for a comfortable future for themselves and those they care about. Heidi is a CFP® professional practicing at an independent registered investment advisory firm in Minneapolis, MN. She also has served as an instructor of employee benefits for some of the largest employers in the country and volunteers as an instructor on financial topics at local high schools. Heidi, her husband Rob, and their two children live in Minneapolis, Minnesota. To learn more about self-wealth visit www.heidihelmeke.com.